for all of you seekers

who know longing

who know thirst

riding through the desert

in search of your Selves

this is for you

From the Back of a Thirsty Camel

Ecstatic Longings

Brandon Thompson

Table of Contents

Ecstatic poetry is a devotional practice which seeks to connect both poet and reader to their innate longing for their essence.

The Local Ecstatics

Preface

I'll never forget the first ecstatic poetry that I read. I could include for you details about where I was at the time, how old I was, who surrounded me, and what I was looking for, but the truth is, none of those things really matter. What matters is what the words did to me, how they came into my heart like lightning bolts. How they woke me up. It was years before the word "ecstatic" would mean anything more to me than an emotion that I felt when I got a good grade on a psychology exam, and yet more years still before I would seriously start writing my own poetry. I didn't know where Rumi was born or when he lived, I didn't know what iambic pentameter was or how many sonnets Shakespeare had written. (And on the latter two, frankly, I still don't.) But herein lies an important distinction for us to recognize together right from the beginning: the transformative power of ecstatic poetry does not require a prerequisite. It does not ask us to be scholars, it does not demand a ground in theory or knowledge, it does not necessitate any past bank of experience. It simply invites us to read, to write, to be curious, and to open to the indomitable majesty of Spirit. Ecstatic poetry is a dance – one of the grandest dances in this life, as best as I can discern. But here is the good news: there are no steps to learn. We need only let the music of our hearts be our guide.

I have been pondering and working with ecstatic poetry for some time now, and it continues to open new doors that I didn't even know were there. It is still surprising me, bringing me to life, helping me to learn about my heart, our world, and the Universe. It is also a maddening mystery, and has, for me, been the catalyst for many a sleepless night spent pacing the floors, trying to unravel the puzzle of my own mind. In truth, there are very few things that I can say about it for certain. However, there is one thing about ecstatic poetry that was apparent to me from the beginning: *longing*.

We all have our longings. They seem to paint a ghostly picture that's woven into the fabric of our lives. Sometimes longing is very much in the foreground, front-and-center, like the unquenchable ache for a lover's kiss. Sometimes longing feels more elusive, nameless, like a splinter in our minds that points toward a void we're not sure how to fill. It was from this longing, this pervasive sense of "something's missing," that my first fascinations with ecstatic poetry began to take root. I was young, just beginning to learn about spirituality, and ecstatic poetry seemed the perfect companion for me as my heart grew. I began to notice that so many poets had been utilizing ecstatic poetry as a *vessel for their longings*: as a way to connect with their core, their essence. In their words, I heard a sacred certainty, as if they were answering some undeniable call at last. And the result? A transformed relationship with their own hearts; an ever-deepening connection to Self.

Longing and essence. Longing *for* essence. If poetry – especially but not exclusively ecstatic poetry – has any power in this world, undoubtedly it is this: to connect us more deeply with our essence, something for which we have been searching our whole lives long.

This book is called "From the Back of a Thirsty Camel." It is a title that I chose, but it is a Path that chose me. The notion of "From the Back of a Thirsty Camel" directly involves our personal endeavors for happiness, our search for meaning, our great quest for love. It also involves the *ways that we fall* along the Way: our missteps, our mistakes, our striving. We get so much wrong, don't we? In our incomplete understanding, we suffer and cause suffering. We act selfishly. We war with ourselves, and those inner wars project outwards, raging across the landscape until the entire world is in peril. Oftentimes, tragically, the story ends right here. We don't go any further, we don't look within, we don't ask why. But this is another mistake. It is just more unclear seeing.

What we get wrong along the Way isn't the all of it. There is a missing piece that begs for illumination. There is also an element of *innocence* about these personal and collective battles. After all, who can be blamed for clamoring, however ineffectively, however desperately, for happiness? For an understanding of love? For the truth about why we are here at all? This does not excuse our behaviors born of ignorance, but instead gives us a way to better understand them as a journey, a deeply-human pilgrimage from not-knowing into Knowing. And the only way to Know is to go on the adventure. This is the very heart of "From the Back of a Thirsty Camel" as an idea, a concept. We're all riding on thirsty camels, through the burning desert of our lives, searching for the one precious elixir that will sate our tongues at last. The path may be marked with many mistakes, false starts, and miraged oases on the horizon. We will fall and rise and fall again. But it is the only journey that will lead us home.

This book tells many tales. Tales of love, tales of longing, tales of cosmic contemplation. From one perspective, it is a deeply-personal journey, an exploration of the essence of Self and Word. I am especially excited to share it with you for a different reason, however. In the end, we are all the same. Though these poems may come from the heart of one poet, I believe there is something in this book that may speak to every heart that opens to its pages.

Will you receive an ecstatic or spiritual experience by reading the poems in this book? Is the aim of ecstatic poetry to induce or provoke you into the ecstatic? On both cases, I would say probably not. The drink that you've been thirsting for cannot be found in a poetry book. But I am here to share with you that, after all I've seen, poetry has the power to show you how to find it for yourself.

Brandon Thompson

August 2015

Invocation

Invocation

i. The Swordsman

the swordsman whets his blade

on a spinning wheel of stone

sparks, red hot fragments

of metal and rock

travel their glowing arc-patterns

and for a moment, he is reminded

of how the stars were born

before returning to his seat

a weathered old oak-stool

pocked with burn marks

for him, an old friend

a living reminder

of the art

of honing steel

in time

his grinding ceases

embers of stonefire cool in the grass

their smoking contrails spiral upwards,

ghostly flower stems,

planted seeds of the swordsman's intent

for the razor-sharpness of his craft

the village stirs

each head hoping to glimpse

the refined gleam of his blade

and he

raising his foil towards heaven

inspects its landscape from hilt

to tip

before sheathing the tool

reborn from its use

to continue the work of the day

steel and stone

streaking comets of superheated matter

but most of all

the will of the man:

not a fighter, nor a lover

but a being-seeing-god

in the most mundane

heaven and earth lie about the swordsman

at his wheel!

the people of the village know,

and throughout the kingdom wide,

that never has lived

a finer poet

than he

Invocation

ii. Prayer

and so it is

that i begin:

words of the ages, come

words of the sages, come

words of truth, be mine this night

that you might set those hearts aflight

which for far too long have held to ground

and might, with love, set skyward bound

come to me, my words of fire

i seek you fullest, my true desire

like the ageless swordsman at his craft

towards the stars i sail my raft

may words i write, my songs of Spirit

fly like sparks, that all may hear it

and fuse sweet heaven and ground below

the two are One, may all men know!

come to me heaven

come to me earth

you two as One

which gave me birth

mantle to mantle and

crust to crust

that my humble words

might raise from dust

sweet new life to deadened ears

as Masters have from ancient years

inspiration is my breath

i exhale words onto the page

where once was darkness, pain, and death

the power of words will light this age

i set these words as solemn prayer

and hold those eyes in tender care

who chance to read and open heart

to this simple swordsman at his art

in silence now, on bended knee

i offer up my sword

that you might hone and forge my heart

i sing my prayer to word

Personal
Prophecies

Personal Prophecies

"We chase phantoms half the days of our lives. It is well if we learn wisdom even then, and save the other half."

~ Mark Twain

We create our own stories, don't we? We forge our paths with little more than the power of our own will and intention. And every so often, in certain magic moments of recognition, we even get to glimpse the beauty of what we can manifest. In one way, on one hand, this understanding seems so solid for us. We say to ourselves: "Of course I'm the captain of this ship. Of course I'm the architect of my own experience." It just makes sense. But maybe you have also noticed that coming to believe in our own power, really owning it and learning to use it as a force for change in our lives, is a long and arduous road indeed. How is it that these two can coexist simultaneously: this deep and abiding awareness of our own power and the ongoing struggle to really actualize it, live it, reside with it? This struggle can soon begin to feel like a chase, as our egos, in their disbelief and desire to control, continually attempt to stifle the wisdom of the Greater Selves within us.

A question has long burned in my heart: *who profits from the prophets?* For years I felt like it would be the perfect line to begin an epic poem about the ways in which we, both personally and societally, misuse the great and potent wisdom left behind by the Masters that we all revere. (After all, who doesn't love a discourse about contemporary distortions of ancient ideas?) The mission to bring this notion into the world felt so important that it was strange to me how, after all the time that passed, the right poem just wouldn't appear. Perhaps it was all too cynical.

It wasn't until I began to take a look at my own writing, my own art, that something else began to emerge, a new realization built on old ideas. An *illusionment*. A reenchantment. I began to see that in my collection of poetry stood a number of writings that, whether I knew it at the time or not, contained a vast amount of power to create change in my life. In fact, through the lens of hindsight, it became clear to me that I was shaping – almost predicting – throughout a years-long journey of personal writing, precisely where my feet would land next. I began to see that no matter who we venerate as the Wise Master of our Times, be it Jesus or Buddha or the bearded teacher at the new-agey yoga center down the street, we are our own prophets. This is so for all of us, excepting none. The truth is, I stumbled upon this idea. I learned it for myself through the vehicle of ecstatic poetry writing, even though I have been told this truth a hundred times before…even though, behind the frosted-glass of my mind, I knew it all along.

The collection of poems in this section, then, are subconscious evocations. They are fortune-teller myths that came true. They have been arranged here as the intentional tale of one poet's journey: from a brash invitation into a tunnel of personal darkness to a reemergence into the light. Have I learned any wisdom along the way? I don't know. What is wisdom but a deeper and more willing embracing of bewilderment with the human condition? Will the pieces, the fragments, of my own intimate journey yield riches for you along your own Path? This is my wish, but it will be for you to decide for yourself.

May we all come to understand the power of our personal prophecies, and learn to wield our prophesizing for the benefit of self, others, and the world.

Dark Heart

where are you

dark heart

sometimes i wonder

if i know you at all

no one can ever fully believe

that you dwell not

in my life

but maybe they're right

tonight

let darkness have me

so that i might come to know

whatever i must

to become a full

awakened

human being

The Half-Breed Poet

i am not a poet

or at least

i don't feel like one

poets live their lives boldly

opposing establishment

opposing the corrupt

opposing others who,

through the eyes of poets,

are exposed for their blindness

at last

i oppose too

but do it more silently

with tinier confidences

unsure of my voice

but sure

unshakable

on the following matters:

establishment is rarely on our side

no matter how ardently some may argue

that they are

corruption is real

and is more poisonous by far

than the poisons that run

in our rivers

which establishment would have us

ignore

and blindness

the blindness of others

who look into our lives and judge without

compassion

or hesitation

and speak with forked tongues

despite their preachings

against speaking with forked tongues

this blindness –

if it continues to be indulged

and enabled

and perpetuated

by blind and sighted alike –

this blindness

will destroy more than lives

it will destroy our world

it is already happening

i am not a poet

or at least

i don't feel like one

but i am not blind

Word's Fall

i could waste your time talking about their colors

and how tragically we take for granted

the holy things that leaves do

in the autumn time

but if you want to read a poem

about the miracles of the earth

i hear mary oliver is really nice this time of year

and anyway

she'd just show you a new way to see

what's already outside

your back door

instead i'm interested in the dance

and what makes those leaves that fall

in the instant that i pass by

choose to fall

for me

the tug of the wind

and months-long lack of water

in their veins

they snap away, free from their home

it can't all be by chance

but chance is a player

too

words for me fall short these days

but one day in mid-october

on the sunlit path towards home

the falling leaves whispered into my ear:

"we're dying now

it's our purpose to nourish the earth

but here's the truth:

in the springtime

you'll see us again"

words fall

short

maybe it's by chance

or for some greater purpose

and in the springtime

i'll know for sure

The Hero's Journey

i never thought i dwelled in darkness

but maybe i have

fooling myself, a sad old man

a specter-in-the-shadows

dreaming of the light

telling everyone who comes to visit

a well-written story

on postcards sent from sunny beaches

but the writing on the back

is ink spills and tears –

"wish you were here

wish i was too"

when i was a boy

my days were filled with adventures

and love

action figures and mother's kisses

i suppose, if they are lucky,

that's what most children get

but fear, the starving stalking-wolf,

was searching in the shadows

constructing the high walls

of this hidden, lonely fortress

here is what i've learned

during the long and painful climb

to the top:

grandest construction

the psyche of each human being

never was born

even the finest architect

who could wish to glimpse the total design

of his own mind

buttresses and pillars

columns built for a king –

but the gargoyles with snarling

red eyes

threaten onlookers

and if the hero wishes to take

the elevator to the top floor

he'll have to slay them

with the sword of his own courage

The Cost of Longing

longing and beauty are not separate

and this is why i grieve

not because all phenomena

are fleeting

for even withered beauty

tells a tale

that lives on

not because of separation

the illusion that we all purchase

with the limited currency of our hearts:

before long

the account is drained

and what remains for us

is a type of bankruptcy

that makes the whole world seem mute

on all the long days

filled with music

no, it is none of these

i grieve because there are those

who perceive the longings of the world

as a sickness –

who misconstrue longing

as the activity of an un-whole heart

seeking its completion

in all the wrong places

what is the cost of longing?

it depends on what you do

when you feel its pull

but should you choose

to ignore it completely,

you will risk missing

the voyage

that could bring you

home

The Burn

i have been a captive

of these uncertain days

and there are few things

that i can say for certain will remain

when this burn is quelled

to ash

i'll find their sootprints in my heart

memories of goodness

and will be reminded that the burn

was never about what would stay

but what was being seared

away

in the laser-light of pain

and suffering

i made my mistakes, and you

were the laundry-lister of my life

but here is what i've decided:

no matter what can be said

or who is doing the saying,

no matter how many wrongs or rights

i have done or haven't,

a human heart has certain

unshatterable chambers

and others that can break

over and over again

without ever falling

into disrepair

it's okay

i can be the only one who tells the tales

of my own worth

this was your strongest message

from the beginning of it all

and i have profited at last

from all of your knifeblade prophecies

so let it burn

and may i arise at the end

with all of the light

and leave those cinders

on the long path

behind

The Starving Soul

or

Berea Beloved

the stars look down

past those mountain-peaks

and smile upon this little town

they show us the bounty that

lays before us:

we can eat like kings

and my soul

is starving

so give me more!

give me more of those djembe-nights

circled around the fire we built

with highs shooting past

the tallest firespark

as drumbeats of kindred kindness

pound my heart

until sunrise

give me more of her gypsy-blue eyes

and the dirt in her fingernails

when she glances over her shoulder

and finds me through the crowd

on a sweaty

summer

night

give me my brothers –

explorers all

the men with full beards and no answers!

then give me their communion

which splices

the atoms of my mind

on someone's back porch

in the moonlight

give me those hills and

the trails that wind around them

to rocky cliffs

on days when the clouds could catch me

if i jumped

give me more of that music

the banjo serenades!

those ancestor-anthems that taste like

garden vegetables and tobacco –

it is not by chance

that the dulcimer is so named

because it is the sweetest sound

there is

yes! this is my home!

so give me more of the things that matter

far less of the things that don't

and open my eyes

to the bounty

so that i may live richly in this place

though my pockets

are always empty

for coin

Love Yourself

love yourself

not because i said you should

or because your dearest ones

have always told you

that it was good

advice

love yourself instead

because you have accepted

that there are many yous

inside the One

and you have seen beauty and beast

the folly of your own darkness

generosity and pride

kindness, cradling, and fear

all of these

because you have felt the sting

of your own selfishness

as it spreads across the face

of someone who loves you

and you have realized

that the only way to be free

of the painful circling

is to love every part —

each You

you see —

like a newborn child

just emerging

from its source

The Wounded Healer

great paradox –

or is it? –

that those who choose

to spend their lives

healing

are those who

have the most to heal

wound runs deep

and calls us onward

first to understand,

next to bandage and salve,

then to stitch

with the loving, golden thread

of the milk of human kindness

we are each of us

unsure surgeons

for the hardest thing is to love

the parts of ourselves

that we would rather

hate

but the healer knows

that if he is to be of any benefit

to the world

that power is born

when he begins to heal

himself

The Time Has Come to Speak of Love

The Time Has Come to Speak of Love

"If you had the courage and could give the Beloved His choice, some nights, he would just drag you around the room by your hair, ripping from your grip all those toys in the world that bring you no joy. Love sometimes gets tired of speaking sweetly, and wants to rip to shreds all your erroneous notions of truth."

~ Hafez

What can be said of a love poem? More specifically, what could possibly be said in a love poem that hasn't already been noted thousands of times by thousands of poets? The shelves in the bookstore are saturated with love poems. We've all heard the same Top Ten Sonnets so many times that we literally revulse when our poet-friend opens up his book to share another of his all-time favorites. "Shall I compare thee to a summer's day?" How about "Shall I mercifully spare thee from another few lines, incessantly grasping for something new to say about love?"

We are sick to death of love poems. I am too.

And yet I continue to write them. Why? Because something is missing. All of us sense it, even without looking too deeply. We are chronically unsatisfied with love in nearly all of its myriad appearances throughout our lives. Its existence seems marked with striving, disappointment, even failure. Our culture is so dense with our collective quest for love that it generally operates in the background now, a shadowy character on the periphery of consciousness. It guides our behaviors, chooses our partners for us, and beckons us ever closer to the sugary, unsatisfying meal-of-love that the television commercials would have us choose. How did we let this happen? Why does it continue to plague us so? Surely *something is missing* in all of our talks of love. But what?

The poems in this section are not your grandparents' love poems. Neither will you find them framed on the walls of your childhood home, where your parents, in their sincerity and desperation, struggled despite themselves to teach their children something real about love. The words that you will read here are risky business. Some of them speak tendernesses, but seek to remind us that love can be freed from the confines of conditioning: that love, in its truth, connects us to the Divine. The real missing piece, though, are the questions we are too afraid to ask. Where do we go wrong with love? What is getting in the way? What are the things that love is – and what are the things that love is *not?* And if we are continually acting out the old ways that have taken root within us since childhood, mustn't there also be a New World Love that might blossom and reach to the sky?

The common path that we all walk towards love might appear to us as the right way, the one that makes the most sense, the one most apparent. But for the most part, we arise from each lover's battle with more questions than answers. More pain than insight. More suffering than joy. Instead of participating in the same old predictable delusions, let us speak of love correctly: as the most powerfully-divine force that there is, as a journey that demands our whole being, as an alchemical fire that can sear away our ignorance. We cannot capture the essence of love from the back of a thirsty camel, so let us rip to shreds all of our erroneous notions of truth…and lead him to the oasis at last.

The time as come to speak of love. And I am tired of speaking sweetly.

The Time Has Come to Speak of Love

the time has come to speak of love

silk woven rose-blankets that cover

our children as they sleep

i can say it no more plainly

than this:

love is the womb that held us

and the spinning heart-center to which

we return

it is the whispered dream

a recollection of ages

an assurance of lives past

recalled when we slumber

for there are none who hold a deeper conviction

than the dreamer who wakes

with words of love

newborn

on her lips

it is the revolving axis

a turning of the wheel

and we

merry-go-round riders

tether ourselves to its bootstraps

even as it turns towards death

there is a hidden certainty

inside the hearts of lovers:

they know they'll be together again

seasons change

in the deep forest fields

where once was barren branch and sky

love arrives and fills each upward gaze

with green

and fragrances –

secret perfumes –

the man who swears

that he's never known love

would in an instant

reconsider

for nothing is more familiar

than the tender scent

he once found

in the bend of his lover's

neck

the time has come to speak of love

but when whispers of the beloved

beg to be spoken

only silence

escapes my lips

My Lover Sang a Song to the Moon

my lover sang a song to the moon

as she searched

with bare feet on wet grassblades

the entire compass

of her heart

but the moon did not appear

still the stars burned

and we watched them together

curious about how light

can penetrate the darkness

and darkness

can hold the light

and when her song had ended

she fell asleep in my arms

at last

and the moon shone

on a moonless night

in an entire sleeping world

all that remained

was the moon

my lover

and i

Beachwalking

if there's one thing you taught me –

and you taught me more than a few –

it's to take my shoes off

when i'm at the ocean

and let the sand drink in

my willing toes

in a world where so many

rush to the beach

to get sun-baked for the summer fashions

you told me that each granule

was a prayer

that reminds us

of our place among the stars

our love broke both of our hearts

but that doesn't change

the light behind your eyes

when you laughed at me

for keeping my shoes on

at the shore

when i was with you

i felt like i was dying

but today i walked along the beach

for the first time since we said

good-bye

and realized that you were teaching me

how to live

A New World Love

i. Causation

wouldn't it be nice

if every child was given

all of the keys

to all of the doors

that hide away their own freedom?

but this is no more the way

than the baby robin who, newly-hatched,

stretches her wings

and attempts to fly

there is much to be learned

before that first flight

will take her onward

there is an old way

the way your father's father

loved his son with calloused hands

the coaldust and shovel

called to him more deeply

than did the space between

his lover's hips

the way your mother's mother

loved her children

like she loved her dining room table

the perfect geometry of

right-angle placemats

every silver fork

a matter more dire

than her daughter's dreams of fairydust

children don't come simply from mother and father

an aching sigh were it so simple!

we are born instead

into a tangle far older

web of causation that our ancestors wove

a puritan's belt buckle shoes

laced too tightly for the babe to breathe

love brought mother and father together

but human conditioning propagates

like a current across the wire

it reaches out from black-and-white photos

and slips its oily fingers

into the hearts of all

      a breath ageless

unexplained longing for more

thoughts of loving-kindness

spirit sleeps soundly until it awakens at last

is it karma? was it designed this way?

the children don't know

what is certain is the truth

that becomes clear

when they are children no longer:

there is a new world love

ii. A New World Love

our fiction-stories tell us tales

of time travel and

flying cars

that soar from the rooftops of

crystal-built skyscrapers

taller than the clouds and

built on a ladder of progress

that peoples of the past never conceived

of ascending

we marvel at the new world

that we might one day build

with gaping jaws and thirsting tongues –

but what if we have always been wrong

and the New World exists

not without, but

within?

there is a new way

a way that isn't written

in your grandmother's scriptures

but is etched in the hearts

of those courageous enough

to write their own stories

of love

the way he kneels at the altar

of his lover's parted legs

and conducts his worship there:

not even because the two

are held as One

but because his next breath

was meant to be

the smell of her skin

the next sound

the cry of her rapture

the way she

in her mightiness

embraces herself as Divine

and moves through their lives

as the being of light

that was revealed

the moment the veil

lifted

the way the two work as One

to open their hearts

past lifetimes of conditioned *shoulds*

and break the walls

built by their forefathers

blazing their trail

to the new

there is a long and heavy coat

that was stitched in childhood homes

and wrapped around tiny shoulders

as a burden to bear

our whole lives long

but the New World Love

invites this coat to fall

and teaches the children

how to fly

at last

Raindrop

the truest words that can ever be spoken

are the words of a lover

to his love

when raindrops come together

on a windowpane

they do not ask why or how

it is simply what they were born to do

in this limitless cycle -

no birth, no death -

that makes the oceans fall

as rain

on the hills and valleys

of our hearts

for on these fire-and-water days

when my lips ache to touch yours, beloved

like the flower aches for her sunlight

i speak my words to you and recognize

that they are somehow more than truth

they are prophecy

of what is yet

to come

Lover's Rain

or

Lovers Reign

the earth roars and

the sky pours tonight

at my home

the heavens open and

water flows

creating rivulets

that are rivers

running down the city streets

that line

my face

across great space

you are there

with the very same

waters

carving tiny canyons

in your heart

may we meet

carried by these waters

not in the middle

nor where you are

or i am

but where We exist

together

Lost and Found

we all feel lost

don't we?

we hide it behind our beer bottles

and big, thick lines of cocaine

we tuck it away in the warm pools of our

dimpled-smiles and small talk –

it comes through our teeth

like a court-case of certainty

long before we realize

the folly of our claims

the truth is

we don't know what the fuck

we're doing

we all feel alone

and late at night

we feel the sting of loss

and cry for the pain of losing

but let me tell you a secret:

this story is not just yours

this is a tale about what it's like to be born

and live in human skin

it is my story

it is ours —

every single being that you've met —

mother, father, friend, lover

knows, no matter how well-hidden,

what it is like to be lost

when i pause to realize

that we are all the same

i weep for the longing in your heart

and remember all the nights i've cried

only to wake with the sun

and find

that all i'd longed for

was already mine

do not cry into your pillow tonight, beloved

know that we are all lost

and remember

that you'll be found

just as you were the last time

in this great cycle

of birth and death

that takes place

between being born

and dying

Drain the Well

oh, lovers

listen closely to me:

i mourn the loss

of all the sagewords

i once thought

i wrote

no poem was ever as beautiful

as words that are spoken

of love

the world will never have them

no eyes will ever read them

for once these words arise from our lips

their only suitable vessel

are the ears

of our beloveds

and the poet's pen

would drain the well

if he ever tried

to capture

them all

Fire and Earth

a new age begins

when we strip off our clothes

our nametags and labels

and surrender ourselves

to the Truth

our birthright is love

and our roles

no more than characters that we play

however well-intentioned

what matters the most

is naked runs through the woods

our only clothing

is the warriorpaint

that we adorn on cheek and breast and brow

like a head plunged fiercely

into the rush of a waterfall

a battle cry erupts

from the lungs of the goddess

and we emerge

transformed

today

the veils dropped

human denial replaced by fire and earth

burning like sunrays

on fair skinned travelers

but solid like the soil and

wet with vegetation

from the other side of the river

smoke rises from the shore

there is a clearing where fire

meets earth

i'll meet you there

naked

at last

From the Back of a Thirsty Camel

dear one

rest for a moment with me

and i will tell you

a story

the path of the lover

is well-worn

to be sure

but perhaps not as easy

or as smooth

as you might think

rumi wrote his lovesongs

to the beloved

and changed the face

of our world forever

with nothing more than words on a page –

words so profound

and speaking such truths

to hidden places within

our hearts

that we assume

in our incomplete conceiving

that he was more

than just a man

but do you think

that the wine we drink

was never seed

or bud

or vine?

never subject to the thirst of draught

the threatening gale

or the pounding, watery needles

of a rainstorm?

before his life as The Master

he suffered and died a thousand deaths

perhaps every so often

tasting the kiss

that called him home

before returning

to his life of suffering

but even in the shoes

of the man they called

Jalaluddin

for years he strove

and searched

and longed

riding through burning desert

on the back of a camel

that thirsted almost as much

for water

as he did

for the truth

of love

my child, the truth about lovers

is this:

every don juan

leaves a trail of heartbreak

in his wake

every cassanova is a liar

and

for every poet who has finally captured

the essence of the beloved

there are a million poems written

from the back

of a thirsty camel

Thunder and Blazes

or

A Night at the Circus

we know nothing of love

but in these suits of human armor

we are built and conditioned

to pretend

that we are certain

it is a trick so deceiving

that we grow to believe it

ourselves

so many of our potent thoughts of love

are built on a scaffold of fear

we clamor atop it on timid tip-toes

mindlessly crooning our loudest lovesongs

and never looking to the ground below

as we balance our lovers on both outstretched hands

and keep a third securely

piggybacked on our shoulders –

if you think this circus-scene sounds a bit

like a comedy

in a way, no doubt

you'd be right –

but fear is still the master

so driven are we that

we scour the globe

convinced that only another's lips

are suitable to speak

our own words

we drown in the thirst

that is the source of this seeking

but all too often

the dowsing rod finds us at a well

that's already

run dry

i tire mightily

of these lofty poet's tales

grasping in the darkness

for something pretty to tell you

about love

i've no more gems to lay at your feet

for once my pockets were lined with

precious stones and gold

but these years spent caught

in the web of human striving

have turned all of my riches

to sand

if your hands are still stuffed

half-deep into your hot bag of peanuts

you might think that i've turned my back

on love

but really,

i'm just leaving the circus

and as the tent-flap closes –

with songs of Sousa marches still in my ear –

i am left with the same ache in my heart

that i had when i bought my ticket:

i long to know something about love

and to finally be done

with fear

Sonnet - Sirenhorns

the time has come to speak of love

but if this moment has truly come

let us speak together of what is real

and position ourselves fast

with feet firmly planted

as shields which might stay

our illusions

too many poets

on too many days

unendingly wax their songs of love

like blaring sonnet-sirenhorns

they hope to convince us

that their longings can take shape

in our hearts –

what an intrusion! –

but when we look deeply

the wisest of us will find

that all the love-poet is seeking

is to fill his own void

with the crumpled pen-and-paper odes

of yesterday

how do i know that this is so?

because i myself

am the finest ode-maker

that i know

tonight

i lay down my quill and ink

and with them

all of the things i've been hoping

you'd hear me say

tonight

let us talk about the things that love

is not

love is not our ceaseless grasping:

the thousand wanting hands that spring

from our chests

this says far more about what we lack

than what we need

love is not projection

for we can spend a thousand lives

waiting for our lovers to be what we wish

and still have a thousand more

yet to wait

love is not the sugarcane trees

that bear fruit to sate a starving man

his hunger is for his own Self

and no kiss could ever hope

to fill his belly

with God

love is neither savior

nor destroyer

not a respite from ravage

nor an escape from

this world that terrifies us

you were born knowing

that love is simple

but to be free from all of your illusions

of love

you must first have loved

and fallen

Dharma on Fire

Dharma on Fire

"Only to the extent that we expose ourselves over and over again to
annihilation will that which is indestructible within us be found."

~ Pema Chödrön

Dharma is a word, and a concept, shrouded in mystery. And like
all good, beneficial explorations, the more we dive into it, the more it
reveals its beauties and complexities to us. In my heart I hold a
secret, satisfied smile for challenging words, particularly words of
eastern derivation, for they present us in the West with the task of
expanding our minds and pulling away from our narrow, black-and-
white conceptualizations. We are used to being given everything with
its simplest explanation; distilled to its lowest common denominator.
But Sanskrit words (and others of a more mystical, oftentimes
Eastern descent) that appear in our Western lexicon don't generally
work that way. They have no singular definitions. And so, they invite
a bit of challenge, a bit of work. They invite us *deeper*: deeper into
their histories, deeper into hearts of the ancient peoples who first
practiced with them. Ultimately, if we are willing to do the work, they
invite us deeper into ourselves.

What is dharma? Most commonly in our culture, we understand
dharma to mean "teaching." In Buddhism, for example, the dharma
points to a set of teachings, first transmitted by the historical Buddha
and passed down from teacher to student over the course of many,
many generations. Buddhists hold the dharma as more than just a
map of teachings, though, and certainly not as some oppressive list of
indoctrinated "shoulds," sacrifices or penances that we all must make
in order to get some reward later on. Instead, they see the dharma as
a path, a Way, a set of ideas that, when utilized with the right
intention, can lead to a happier, more Awakened life. The idea is that
this has worked for countless individuals over a vast expanse of time,

and we have the blessed occasion, here in this life, to hear the dharma and benefit from its ideas about how to live more peacefully, more gently, more fully. I have been a Buddhist practitioner and teacher for many years, and I can say with great personal certainty that this is so. I prefer to think of the dharma as a set of ideas that might sound true to us, individually, on our own personal paths. They are notions, suggestions, prescriptions – not unlike what a doctor may suggest to salve an aching wound – that can teach us about inner peace, train us in the art of being truly happy.

Okay, so, be honest. At best, all of this sounds a little dry, doesn't it? A brief discussion about word-practice, some information about Buddhism and dharma; it's nothing you haven't heard before. And why all this explanation in a poetry book?

I would say it is time, friend, that we light it all on fire.

The dharma is a means to an end, but it is not the end itself. Its purpose, most succinctly, is to *annihilate* the parts of us that keep us locked inside our own prison, and then, to show us how we might orchestrate a jailbreak. This is a process that scorches the terrain of our preconceptions so that new insights can grow. It is as painful as it is mighty, as terrifying as it is marvelous. We are all travelers on the journey of our own personal dharmas. But in order to uncover our indestructibility, we must first be on fire for change.

These are the words of Path, the songs of a seeker. They are the words of a rebel-Buddhist who long ago grew tired of himself, of the worn-out ways of this world, and of the old, antiquated tactics that so many of us employ in our frantic struggle to wake up. These are the words of the dharma on fire.

Dharma on Fire

the buddhists are looking for me

to be more buddhist

they wonder why i fill my pages

with this intense longing

and love

while they search for a pithy poem

about a cloud

the hard-hearted lovers –

the ones so jaded that

they'd have you believe you should be too –

are concerned that my words

are deluded

they twist their faces

into sour citrus smiles

at the thought

of another sonnet

they'll all think what they will

but if you're reading these poems

and you don't see the dharma-on-fire

well, friend,

i invite you

to look a little closer

Doorstep

do not come to my doorstep

until

you have looked at yourself

through the mirror of your Self

until

you have suffered enough

to know

that suffering is not the way

and have seen

what lies on the other side

of your own confusion

until

you have befriended

that place in you

that judges

because of fear

until

you have conquered your foes:

the poison of greed

and

the need to possess

until

you have found the teacher

the one which dwells

within your own heart

the one which binds you

to the Truth

until

you can speak

through the voice of your heart

and not

through the lens

of your own projections

dear one

my door remains always

open

to all beings everywhere

but

with sadness, i must confess,

it is not a doorway

that you can walk through

still wearing your

prisonclothes

Rhythm

the ants no more ask

why they must travel in their

    tidy

straight lines

concerning themselves

with little more than

the gathering business

of their day

than does the rain as it taps out

its metallic cadences

on the tin roof

    once built

to shelter a human being

from its pour

i sit silently and

observe

as the space between the two

    narrows

and soon there is no separation

between ants and rain

sky and earth

the meditator on her cushion

    breathes

as the maple tree breathes

and the porchlight

    shines

like the heart of a dear friend

if you look

with the eyes of God

there is no separation

it's all rhythm

    all just rhythm

and everything

    is in its place

How to Meditate

let us not overcomplicate the matter:

just watch your mind

notice where it tries to take you

as the multitudinous rivers that pull

at your heart

begin to recede

as you breathe

just notice where the thing called "you"

wants to go

when there's no where to go

but here

and when the squealing child

runs towards the cookies on that high-up shelf

scoop her gently in your arms and say

"my child, my love,

stay with me"

do this over and over

on days with sun and days with snow

until you find that you've become

the master

when before you served only

the whims

that you were once conditioned

to oblige

what is mind?

what is the activity of mind?

what are the habits of mind?

these are the golden three

sit quietly with these questions

for their answers are the keys

to your freedom

just watch your mind every day

while you sit in the refining fires

of your cushion –

make friends with your experience

and please

don't forget

to laugh

Stay

one can learn much

by listening to a rainstorm

have you ever

from beginning to end

sat without ceasing

and let it take you

on its wilding

journey?

at first

the orchestra only tunes

winds and brasses and strings

the rumble so far off

it can scarce be heard

some say they can smell it

on the air

that's the time

when most men run

into the comforting arms

of leather sofas and

frying pan melodies

those who are braver

feel the first foreign droplets of sky

on their necks

but rarely stay with the storm

long enough to watch

water turn soil into

yellow clay puddles

a morning cocktail for treeroots

they drink and smile and stretch

their showered limbs

while the half-brave man decides he's

seen enough, and,

content with himself

finds another distraction:

a god he worships more deeply

than the one just

outside his window

rare is the man

who holds his seat

until the last thunderclap has passed

he is the one who welcomes

the discomfort

of soaking, clinging clothes

who'd rather brave the roaring wind

and stinging pour

than sit in separation

in a sterile dreamland

built

to help us forget

who we are

it is not always easy

to be with a rainstorm

and you will want to run

stay

and listen

as she tells you

all

you need

to know

Two Poems for Seekers

i. Condensation

what's so bad

about being a seeker?

i'll take my longings

and glimpses of God

any day

over the concreted mind

that has it all

figured out

ii. Nowhere

what's so bad

about being a seeker?

i'll take my longings!

they prompt me to unfurl the sail

and travel the yet-known waters

of my heart

your longing has brought so many faces before you

look deeply, dear one, and see

how each of them

has been your most valued teacher,

even when it ended in pain

tell me

how many of man's creations might have never been

without the mighty and mysterious call

of human longing?

i'll take my occasional glimpses of God!

they teach me that i dwell

in but one realm of the real

half-asleep and ever waking

to the next

you will meet those along the way

who would tell you

that all you are seeking

is already yours

but if you are wise, it will be clear

that they're really just in

a big rush

so slow down, seekers!

feel the depth of your longing

and the echoing call of the Divine!

take up your walking sticks

and backpacks full of provisions

for the long journey ahead

recognize with me

that the end of the path

is just something that we create

in our striving

to not be

nowhere

Open Sky

or

Incense Isn't That Bad

the four walls of this room

have seen my silent toiling

for weeks, months

i have my storylines

they sound like

"if i'm going to do my good work

and offer my service

this door must remain shut!

whatever's outside is a distraction"

but something happens

when we shut our doors

unbridled mind becomes calloused thought

and the cranky curmudgeon

armed with judgments and unbudgments

places his feet inside old empty tissue boxes

his toenails grow long and yellow

his mind grows stale

and groans like an old staircase

that abhors the weight

of new climbers

today i opened the door

and felt the rush of earth-wind

that i've heard

but ignored

right outside the windowpane

a gentle force against the stagnant air

of incense perfumes

whose burning i've been justifying

all this time

the storyline sounds like

"i'll burn incense in here

while i do my work

and that will loosen my rock-hard mind"

i realized today that

stepping outside is a lot

like stepping inside

and above my head

there's not a cloud

in the sky

Horseblinders

group sharing is such a lesson:

everybody just wants

their own stories told

it's innocent mostly

i don't think they're selfish

just more victims

of ignorance

the human condition

the larger the group

the more voracious

the horserace

their blinders are on

viewpoints fixed only

on what their riders

want them to

see

but who are

the jockeys

riding these stallions

controlling their desperate

struggle

for supremacy?

it is ego

this is the master

the bondage

the chains

the bridle and saddle

and the rider

himself

Hammock

be homeless with me

let the places within you

that have rarely

found their rest

swing sweetly

in the hammock

i've prepared for you

in the cradle

of my heart

All (who) Wander

it's strange what travelers do

as they come into our lives

and go

we know them when we see them

lover, vagrant, teacher

none of them are here to stay

what is it that awakens

when a traveler crosses our

path?

sometimes

it is their departure

that shows us

where to go next

sometimes

a traveler happens upon our stony,

stagnant lives

and helps us to remember

that we are travelers

too

Marvelous Fear

far-flung were those

our ancestors

who

in the quiet of their lives

gazed upwards at the thunderstorm

and cowered at its rage

they fled for shelter and screamed in fear

certain that some unknown action

had angered the Great Punisher

whose windswept indignation

broke the branches of their homes

and flooded their fields

with waters of vengeance

there were some

though

who looked into the dazzling light-show

of concussion-clouds

and through the pounding of their hearts

found a miracle

that watered the crops

and fed the children

even though it complained for a while

and threatened with a vicious ruckus

the storms always passed:

this was one thing

they could count on

it was the silent moments thereafter

that moved the men to hold their lovers

and the women to cradle the littlest ones

all the more tightly

with tender gazes of gratitude

underneath the clearing skies

of ages past

marvelous fear

the world today is different

but fear has never changed

it rumbles forth from the time eternal

and attacks with cacophonous lies

of its own permanence

such a trickster is fear

that most of us can't recall the truth:

fear is a marvel in our lives

one small facet of the illimitable gem

called consciousness

that joins us immediately

with all beings

for all beings feel fear

fear reminds us that we aren't alone

marvelous fear

fear-as-a-marvel

rarely shall we find a teacher more willing

to pierce our hearts –

not out of vengeance

nor from rage

but with the deepest and most hidden truth of

our Selves

fear is a perfectly-polished mirror

if only we have the courage

to look it in the eyes

do not be afraid, beloved

no matter what

instead

look to the sky and find rapture

in the lightning's flash

take heart

for fear is a dear friend

calling your name

and it can show you

how to be

fearless

Jailbreak

dear one, know this:

if a wise man should whisper to you

that freedom from illusion

is an easy path –

perhaps also that he knows the way –

you have heard only the whispers

of more illusion

and it may be easy to believe

that there are those who prowl your path

with honey on their tongues

one day you will realize

that all of those sweet-speakers

were no more than reflections

of your self

the many faces of your own craving

for a release

from your suffering

you thirst

gazing downward

into the pool of false promises

as countless forms of deception

beg for you to fill your cup

it may take lifetimes of sorrow

to recognize at last

that habit laid the concrete floor

comfort raised the bars

conditioning built the spiral walls

in the wasteland of your prison

and you have been afraid

it is possible to orchestrate

a jailbreak

but if freedom is to be yours

there is but one elixir you must drink:

the golden wine of courage

it is not coincidence

that we consider courage

the opposite of fear

while courage

is the scariest thing of all

so conquered by fear are we

that we drink the sickening

syrup of ignorance

from birth to death

and over again

we know the wish is foolish

hoping

with each passing hour

that today's dip of the cup

will yield the medicine at last

the time will come

when your revulsion with suffering

becomes so great

that you will realize

you have always

had a choice

precious one, choose courage

no matter how afraid you've been

of the green meadows or

the unfamiliar terrain

that you've always glimpsed

through the bars of your

prison-window

the sun will burn your skin at first

and sear your darkened eyes

the winds of foreign lands

will tug your ragged clothes

and scream into your ear

but look over your shoulder

see the hungry crows circling that distant,

rotted tower

in your heart will bloom a lotus

and you will know the truth:

choose courage

and the walls of your prison

will crumble

at your tired,

trembling feet

Projectionist

what would you become

if you could be everything that you are

behind the veil

of your own illusions?

the one you call 'i'

is a thousand still photographs

projected onto a screen

it is a convincing drama

but there is a projectionist

who sits silently

in the booth above

and watches

from behind the spinning reels

today

climb the stairs

and find the One

who shines the light

at the source

Drive All Blames Into One

it seems the whole world

would have you believe

that everything occurs "out there"

the good, the bad

sufferings and joys

the candies and the curses

all belong to that elusive *other*

that exists outside the windowpane

of your own confining

experience of Self

these are the games that we play

to keep the doors locked

but fault and blame

placed out on the front stoop for others to gather

turn us all into the victims

of each drama that unfolds

and we can spend our lives there

as the sole casualty

of every war

we wage

responsibility is freedom

but we'd rather be behind bars

oh, dearest one,

don't you see?

nothing really happens to you

all phenomena happen *at* you

and you alone decide

where to go

from there

Guru With a Wounded Heart

i'll never forget

who i was then

i see him now

through the lens of

presentmind:

he was emerging

in all the ways

that the word might depict

it was the birth of his heart

and his eyes

perfectly open

predictably naïve

were beginning to see

for the first time

he thought he owed it

all to you

guru

oh, how you hated the word

you told us all

that wasn't what you were

if you meet the Buddha

on the side of the road, kill him

but none of us felt

that you deserved to die

today i remembered

the moment i understood

what you'd been trying to tell us all along

you spoke of woundedness

as if we should have known exactly

what you meant

and you cried

for the misery of the world

without ever

shedding a tear

it took some time for it to

appear

and did so slowly in my Being

as petals bud

not immediately, but slowly

purposefully

reminder of some Greater Design

it was my ego that i'd turned into

my enemy

it was myself

versus my Self

in a war of subtleties

my own war, a microcosm

of the wars raging inside the hearts of men

as i in my ignornance

strove for Awakening

i had misunderstood

those modern translations

of ancient Truths

but when i began

to experience my ego

as my wound

that was when everything

began to change

and i remember your face

when you realized my softening:

we celebrated

the beginning of the end

of the war

together

i recognize that your time left

here among us

grows brief

and sitting with you

at least for me

is a gift i may never

have again

may all Beings come to understand

precisely what you mean by

"wound of the heart"

this includes me

The Riddle

The Riddle

"Don't search for the answers, which could not be given to you now, because you would not be able to live them. And the point is to live everything. Live the questions now. Perhaps then, someday far in the future, you will gradually, without even noticing it, live your way into the answer."

~ Rainer Maria Rilke

I am up late at night, the moon is hidden by the clouds. I am pacing fervidly, wringing out my hands, outside on my back porch in the hanging-dampness of the darkness. The porchlight shines, a knifeblade of illumination resting on the kitchen table of my consciousness. I know that I am a poet, and that ecstatic poetry is my calling. But I don't even know what an ecstatic poem is. I try to write it. I know it's a riddle, a conundrum, a puzzle. It throbs in my chest and my fingertips. It has to come out; it aches for its answer. And here's what's most maddening of all: the riddles all tell me that I already have their solutions…but it's up to me to discover them on my own.

What is ecstatic poetry? This is the question that incites a bare-knuckle brawl in the arena of my mind. A late-night, hair-pulling, manic longing without beginning or end. A crazed alchemist's laboratory filled with words and ink and pages. Sometimes the infuriating mystery of it all brings me to my knees. Other times, the Words and I stay awake until sunrise, tangled in my bedsheets and giggling like children.

I suppose it's just like any good love story.

One could say that this section contains poems that seek to answer the question "What is ecstatic poetry?" This is the riddle that I have been trying to solve for years. What feels truer for me, though, is that this section tells the *real* story, gets to the essence of all of my grappling, my love affair with this practice that can transform our hearts. Some of the poems in this section may read like nonsense. Others are my direct attempts to find the words that might unlock the riddle at last, not just for me, but for all of us who feel in our hearts the transformative power of words. Have I succeeded? That isn't the point. Poetry is all about our freedom, and ecstatic poetry, as a devotional practice, is one way that we can point ourselves, steer the ship, in the direction of what we have been searching for. I haven't discovered much during my midnight crusades out on the back porch, but this I can say for certain.

This is the question that I have been living. These are the ravings of a mad scientist. This is one poet's ongoing dance with the riddle of poetry. Let us dance together for a time and, together and separately, see if we can live our way into our own answers.

Birth of the Artist

i once read that

art is pain

that might be true for some

but i prefer to think

that art is longing

after all

what is pain

but longing

for the truth?

we would be wise to understand

that longing can create an illusion:

a faulty sense of separateness

between one's beating heart

and the waking, walking world

you might come

to a different conclusion, but

after all i've seen,

it seems that the greatest art is made

by those who hold their longings

like the reluctant parent

who didn't really want this child

but knows as well

that the greatest gift they will ever leave

emerged the day

she

was born

Conversation

conversation:

"are you a poet?"

"yeah."

"you don't just come across a poet every day."

"well, brother, let me tell you"

Instruction

to be a poet

don't get caught up

in trying to say something

instead, remember:

god is always speaking

though it is not with your ears

that you will hear

his voice

A Secret

let me tell you a secret:

poetry is born

from that ache in your chest

it might feel like a question,

but the truth is, it's the answer

A Poem Is

i.

a poem is a riddle

that knows

you have its answer

be still

and god will whisper the truth

into your ear

ii.

a poem is a riddle

that knows

you have its answer

but when you begin your fervent seeking

all the voices begin to whisper: "be still"

iii.

i toiled for years

trying to find a way to tell you

what a poem is

i knew that it was a riddle

and i knew i had its answer

but if you're out to sea

and can't see the ocean waves on the shoreline

i don't know if my pointing finger

can serve you

from this boat

Morning Plea

stay asleep, my love

let the drowning warmth of slumber and pillow

continue to sing

its song to you

last night we made love

by the fire, then slept

let me imagine

as the sun rises

that you are still there

in that place

where nothing can harm you

this morning, i rose early

with a screaming tidal

of words

eroding the shore

of my consciousness

don't wake just yet, beloved

i have to sort this all

out

solve the riddle

that threatens to drive

this poet mad

and i'm no good to either of us

until what's inside

finds its way

out

Ode to Winter

oh winter

i can feel your reluctance

but we both know

that your days

are numbered

so if you can find it in your heart -

that heart

that's normally filled with

icyroad morningdrives

frozen pipes depriving bathtubs

of their glug

and winterclothes

like prisonclothes that

hide the best parts of us away -

listen:

i miss my back porch

and poems written

at my kitchen table

are the worst kind

of shit

Coffeeshop Blues

how many poems have been written

about raindrops

rolling down a windowpane?

how many poems have been written

about the Self?

i used to be able to churn out a dozen

of each

over a cup of coffee

but now it's time to write about

things that really matter

we've been here for hours

and i haven't said even the first thing

i sat down

to tell you

but that's okay

it's at about this point

in every poem

when i get lost

anyway

Eavesdropping

i hear you speaking

about the razor's edge

fearless in the face

of your own uncertainty

i watch as your wisdoms

work on me

as the skillful baker fills my pantry

and nourishes the places within

that were hidden

even from themselves

i bow to your courage

fierce and noble as

the wolf pack

blossoming like a single

rose

against the odds

of its nighttime birth

if it is true

that fire meets earth

with no space between the dirt

and the heat

it must also be true

that a journey to the pinnacle

of Self

is a harrowing metaphor

for the letting go

that is to come

it is a vulnerable

raw

and tender leap

into the river under the suspension bridge

but the power of your words

finds us all

in the desert

of your lovemaking

break all the rules, beloveds!

poetry

is all about

your freedom

If You Love a Poet

in the end

there remains a final riddle

that has ache

to be unraveled

but let me tell you, friends,

this poem isn't going to solve it

you look into these words

and what you see is my journey

a record

of life

and loves long past

a flash-frozen monument

amid the snowy landscape

of longings that you suppose

yet linger in my chest

you mistake

those epitaphs etched on pages

for the places i must still be

a falsely-living truth

inside your made-up mind

but from this perspective, i wonder

which of us is the one

still trapped

by stagnant ideas?

if you love a poet, be warned:

his library hasn't burned

as did that egyptian marvel

that once held the limitless wisdoms

of the ancient world

and there you will find the tales

of all his bygone journeys

if you love a poet, he will show you

the miracles meant only

for you and he

and yet you will live in a world

where the past lives

on your bookshelf –

please do not mistake the present

for the enduring record in his wake

for the poet's mind is always changing

ungraspably

from the old world

to the new

Quantum Self

Quantum Self

"Some part of our being knows where we came from. We long to return, and we can, because the cosmos is also within us. We're made of star stuff. We are a way for the cosmos to know itself."

~ Carl Sagan

From the birth of this illimitable faculty that we know as human consciousness, we have looked to the stars and wondered about our place among them. Our ancestors revered the heavens with equal amounts of awe and fear: they marveled at the mystery of the changing sky and trembled helplessly underneath its power. Over the centuries, our legends were born. Not only did the universe literally give rise to our planet and our physical bodies, but in our early relationship with the natural world, we co-participated in the creation of a collective consciousness, a vast compendium of stories and myths for a world that we could not yet otherwise explain. This exists, and influences our lives in limitless ways, to this very moment. It is interesting how we have assigned meaning in this way: for both inner and outer phenomena. The Greek and Roman Gods and Goddesses of ancient lore both dwelled in the heavens as celestial beings *and also* represented primordial, base attributes of consciousness: love, power, truth, beauty, wisdom, justice. Our systems of astrology, based solely on the stars and planets, can tell us far more about our minds and personalities than can even the most efficacious psychological inventory that we have developed. We are beings of both heaven and earth, quantum and unquantifiable, and starving for an understanding of how it all came to be.

It was not until most recent few moments in human history that we truly began to sate this hunger. Our modern sciences have revealed to us the unspeakable wonders of the universe in which we reside, finally providing us with the tools needed to answer the greatest questions of our existence. More than ever before in the history of humanity, we now know the immeasurable scope of the cosmos. We have realized the immensity of time. We have seen the holy parallels between galaxies and atoms. We've discovered that every tiny last bit of us was once forged, tempered, created in the furnace of a star. In short, science has offered us unquestionable proof that the universe exists within us. We are *literally* star stuff. We are the essence of the cosmos, and the cosmos is the essence of us.

But something still remains. We have a base, innate, undeniable longing to return to that essence, to understand it, to embody it. Each of us feels this longing, all of us, everywhere; this is the human condition. It is the very reason why our ancestors turned their gaze to the heavens and created their powerful, archetypal tales, the legends that still live in our hearts. And today, in the present, we have the precious opportunity to know more, see more, expand more than in any other period of the past. In all of my considerations, I can think of no miracle more profound than this.

The poems in this section are inspired by this miracle, by the majesty and might of the cosmos and our place within it. They ask the questions that we are able to ask now; they explore frontiers that are both ancient and also imbued with the fresh perspective of recent discovery. What is consciousness? Where did we come from? And what is this thing known as "love" that occurs when star stuff meets other star stuff? Ecstatic poetry is a practice of connecting with our essence, coming to understand it more deeply; therein lies its power to awaken, to transform. And from this perspective, these poems are the humble offerings of but one poet on the path: just another way in which the cosmos is coming to know itself.

Every last being on this tiny planet is a seed of the stars. May we each of us grow tall on this cosmic stage as we unravel the mystery of quantum self.

Quantum Self

what is a thought that is more meta than meta?

and when it comes

from where does it arise?

let me propose a word to you:

quantum

quantum beyond meta-ness

is a billion atomic tongues

breathing heart-words into your ear

so that the self beyond the Self

existing three-folds away from

the one you call "me"

speaks

what then, do we hear?

the sages say that the word is "om"

what i hear sounds more like

everything

the world carries out

its busy life in a business suit

inside the briefcase are thoughts

of separation

but when the veil is moved aside

the vastness

between hearts narrows

and in the far-off galaxies

entire civilizations lift their eyes

to the stars

this is the spark that lights

the quest

for knowledge

who wrote this poem

as i was falling asleep beside you?

the one who is neither you

nor i

nor even us —

it is the thousand-pointed

one called "we"

the quantum mechanic behind

the locked door

it is difficult to feel

that you are a part

of an infinite Universe

from this diminutive dot in the blackness

but look at the place behind

your thoughts

and see that there is no distance

between Self

and the cosmos

Stop Running

how wide do we have to expand

before we realize

that the Universe is inside

and we can stop running

trying

to catch it

Starseed

i once heard that

life began on earth

by seeding:

an ancient orbital bombardment

the stork came

those eons ago

and left his seeds

planted in burning proto-soil

now

we live and thrive

awareness born of matter and atoms

can you think of a greater

miracle?

we opened our eyes and marveled at the sun

and grew to find

that it is but one drop in a sea

the power of science

has shown us these wonders

but no wonder is greater than love

the titans that govern the cosmos

are as nothing

when i realize

that god lives in you

and me –

that once was planted

the seed of the stars

which breathes when you breathe

and kisses when we

kiss

there are riddles

that even science

can't solve:

where lives the soul?

who is this consciousness?

and why do these apparitions

choose to love one another

on this dust-speck world, itself

once randomly birthed

by chance?

the answer is a word

that we have created

this well-intentioned cosmic consciousness

trying to explain itself

to itself

the word is "god"

and god lives

within these mysteries

that we may never

fully

unravel

The Waking

i notice how often i write

about the Universe –

spinning, churning, whirling

limitless –

because the word

love

isn't big enough by far

to encompass the vast expanse

of human loving

we tiny beings

riding on this rock

have access in our hearts

to something far greater

than all that can be seen by our eyes

and known by the power

of our sciences

but i tire of talks of

the Universe

for even it

from star to galaxy

to great cosmic web

dares not be considered

when i remember your skin

under my hands

and your voice

in my ear

so let us remember

that this story is not just ours

instead

we are on the grandest journey

of them all:

to learn to love

and to one day wake up and realize

that love is far larger

than the distance from human hearts

to the farthest star

in the night

sky

Star Stuff Meeting Star Stuff

born of the cosmos

but returned at last to

one another:

star stuff

meeting star stuff

and burning as we once did

when our atoms were a sun

this is how it is

when two hearts

come together

you should know, dear one,

that love lives on

for far longer than it has taken

the molecules within a star

to become living flesh

and blood

The Question of Consciousness

night has fallen, and

the sky

is cloudless

there is a Knowing that we cannot

explain:

it compels us to raise our heads

to those familiar old burning-globes

that dot the blackness

with their taunting tongues –

they beckon us closer

despite the impossibility

of their desire

we become aware that we can only visit them

in our imaginations

and this is when the real questions begin:

what is it that imagines?

where did we come from?

why are we here?

and most desperately of all,

we burn to know *who*

is doing the asking

the collective sigh of human lives

breathes the words:

"what is consciousness?"

what is it that loves

that cries

that is born

and dies

and looks outwards

from behind these eyes

to ponder poignantly

at the skies?

this poet asks too many questions

for the answer is spinning

in wild circles

in the atoms that teach my heart

to beat:

it is the universe that inquires

when our tongues speak

each question

the cosmos has infinitely sung

its curiosities into the void

but needed human ears

to hear

its music

night has nearly ended

and a new morning always comes

so let us say it simply now:

consciousness is just stardust

that goes by my name

perhaps this is something

that we can all agree on

and let all of our questioning

bring us closer

to the stars

A Breath Ageless

A Breath Ageless

"Dragged and pulled in love, I bear all the pain. Caught in this confusion, in this bitter sweetness, I am the captive of this journey. It is the scent of home that keeps me going, the hope of union, the face of my Beloved. I know our fate is separation, but until my last breath, I will search for my sweet love. I will seek my home."

~ Rumi

What is the story of A Breath Ageless? To hear the fullness of the tale, you'll have to become comfortable with a healthy measure of contradiction.

Once upon a time in my life, a wise friend would often say "We're never just one thing." For me, this idea represented a pivotal transformation of what I understood about human nature. Our minds are conditioned, habituated, to prefer consistency and dependability, and when we don't get what we're after, we harden, we attack, we project, we suffer. When this happens, the only result is further chaos. I often wonder how our lives and our world would change if only we could find a way to abide in a deeper truth: we are infinitely complex, perfectly beautiful constellations, living and breathing expressions of the yin and yang, the both/and. We are both fearful *and* fearless, demonstrating, at different times and in different situations, both cowardice and courage. We are taught by our culture to be self-centered, but in the rawest parts of our hearts, we are innately selfless. Each human life is a continual dance with the tidal forces of the both/and, an invitation to embrace contradiction, uncertainty, and to learn to soften into an understanding that we are "never just one thing." I believe that this practice applies especially to love.

A previous section in this book brought us on a journey into the groundedness of love, the struggle of love. Questions were explored like "What illusions do we hold that keep us separated from love?" and "What are the things that love is not?" If that section held the earth-principle of love – the cutting yang and realism that are necessary for us to recognize if we are to achieve a complete picture of love – then the idea of A Breath Ageless speaks on its heaven-principle, its softness, its sensuality, its yin. Love is a maddening contradiction that drags and pulls on us our whole lives long. In love, we find one of the most potent expressions of the both/and in the entirety of human experience. To say it all in another way, we would be wise to remember that we cannot have a complete conceptualization of our world without looking to both earth and heaven for our answers...and so it goes with love.

Do you remember what it feels like to fall in love? Even the greatest cynics cannot wholly discount its rapture, the glimpse of God that we are all afforded when at last a lover looks into our eyes and, perhaps without even uttering a word, tells us "I see you, I know you, I love you." Lovers *breathe agelessly* into one another's lives: as if the power of love transcends even time, they seem to know that they've loved before.

If thoughts of love evoke a hardening for you, or a sense of loneliness or loss or sadness, that is okay. Love so very rarely takes up permanent residence in our lives. This section invites you to recognize, though, that there is something behind the darkened veils of all of our striving. There, we find that the breath of love is ageless, and that each of us are pilgrims on the path, seeking the face that calls us home.

Ripple

it's taken me this long to realize

that the act of loving –

the exchange of sacred communion

that singularly honest

act of surrender –

ripples

making love is not just one finite series

of moments

over and done with

and discarded

at the end

it is an act of

creation

one night with you

your flesh at my fingertips

your breath in my ear

your quivering voice

gives rise the oldest tales ever told:

no matter what forms these ancient consciousnesses have taken

throughout the epochs

since time eternal

these tales

pouring from your lips

have burned in the hearts of men

since first we woke up in this place

and began to love

and then

at last

the holy explosion

the Universe begins again

between your thighs

right there

in that place where we meet

the birthplace of all worship –

the only churchhouse

that has ever shown me the face of God –

as your body does

what it was born to do

and together

we begin to understand

that miracles are far more commonplace

than we had once

imagined

it is these moments, all

they take up residence in my heart

and there they stay

the days that follow

are ghostly dreams

and i'm really nowhere

but right there

still

with you

Song of Waves

there is a time

for disconnection

when the selves that we once knew as whole

glance back at us when we turn from

  the mirror

we could swear their eyes

speak longing

we question

  why?

what decisions were made

what signs did we miss

to have found ourselves so estranged

that even our own blessed bodies

feel more foreign

than the aching taste of another's

  kiss

here is the truth:

    it's all just waves

eroding places that no longer serve

it is painful, beloved

but take heart

for it is neither sand nor stone

that the waves are churning

instead, they are showing us how to wash

    ourselves

of ourselves

there is a time

for different waves to form

a co-created union

of flesh

and sweat

    conjured waves of breath

expand and contract

and to your surprise

your naked legs wrap even more suitably

around your lover's waist

than do your arms

    around his neck

here are the crests

and there the troughs

they flourish outward from that place inside

that is the earth

    that is the stars

where he

        meets you

            and you

                meet him

it isn't even a meeting

as much as a recognition

do not waste your time

on these tired old words

and don't let your head be spun

    or seduced

by the silly little

    gimmick

        that poets use

            to make their verse

look like ocean waves

    on paper page

instead, dear one,

trust

that alienation is always temporary

and ride the waves

together with him

and all alone

on the long and sacred journey

back home

Beauty is an Idea

beauty is an idea

born in the breast

a symphony of rose petals

that swirl and inspire

inviting the eyes to feast on their perfume

but we've made a fine mess

of it all

haven't we?

in our legends

ancient texts point a broken arrow

towards truth

a face once launched a thousand ships

but war

is the opposite

of beauty

within these starving selves

of candy-coated desire

we look towards one another

and find either beauty or revulsion

so rarely recognizing

that both are mirrored images

of self

i want to tell you

that you are so beautiful to me

and not choke on the words

or fear your disdain

because of how horribly we have corrupted

this idea

called beauty

Eskimo Kisses in the Springtime

the season came and went

i swear i was present

in every instant

but like the wind

it stayed for but a moment

and brushed my face

with your lips

before moving on to the next town

to sing its songs

from their rooftops

i knew it wouldn't last

forever

there was fire

and glances that knew my heart

from across a smoky bar

and through the crowd

and noise

and booze

i gazed back at you

drinking in each moment

i knew then

that i should linger

because all seasons change

the music played loud

in my living room

even a poet

would find it hard to capture

the sacred things that we felt –

somehow for one another –

when another song

yet another song

spoke to the very same place

in my heart and yours

chances were taken

and seeds planted

that grew tall

and bore the fruits

of love

tender as the tip of your nose

on mine:

eskimo kisses

like my mother once gave

i couldn't believe it was you

punctuating the moments after

our lips had finally given in

to their hunger

for one another

it was the springtime, love,

and we were born with the trees

the birds sang

that morning i held you

but all seasons change

Honesty

last night

i was too drunk

to tell you how i

really feel

that

your skin is like god to me

the face i never thought i'd touch

when i was a boy

dreaming of the day

when i'd touch the face that called me home

and yours now

this moment

cradled in my palms

i cannot imagine that i will hold

even the face of my child

with more tenderness

or lovingkindness

or awe

that

your breath comes

expanding and contracting

like the cosmos

an entire Universe

from birth to death

is like one breath

in the eyes of god

and there you were

in my arms

breathing the fire of the moment

a perfect mirror

for all the lessons

humanity

has not yet learned

Takeoff

what is this manic madness

that pours through my mind

seeping its way

into even the purest

and well-intentioned

thoughts?

just now

i was saying a prayer

for the safety

and well-being of this airliner

full of passengers

and was interrupted by throbbing thoughts

in rhythm with my heartbeat

of my soft, wet home

between your legs

Morningsong

i remember

the morningbirds singing to us

outside in the dark

it was early spring

and the swiftest flyers

had just returned

to remind us that

the night

was coming to an end

long ago

mary jane had her

last dance

a dance that brought fire

to my fingertips

and aching

all over your body

the couch that held us

replaced by a bedroom

and magic cocreated

by the only real dance

there is

i was drunk

but no longer on drink

or smoke

i was drunk like Rumi was

the day he met Shams

and you were naked

underneath the bathrobe

that hung five sizes too large

over your shoulders

and you pulled me

in

closer

no space would do

no substitute for my arms

and your smile spoke

playfulness and fire

sweetest contentment

but bliss

above all things

and you pulled me closer

i remember

what it felt like

to be wanted

even after all the wanting

had been ours

i had hoped to write

about the love that we made

before the birds began their song

to the dawn

but that would require a poet

far greater than i

instead

i can only speak

in hushed whispers

and fading memory

of the twice-clouded bliss

that two hearts knew

before

the morningsong

Ineffability

standing there

beside the fire

i said to you

that

you were like a poem to me

and then

i came to my instruments

and began to write

nothing

Kiss

the world

but more

the Universe and God

whoever she is

are always on your lips

when you speak

and when we sing together

the songs we sang when we

were young

but kissing you

is more than both to me

as we breathe together

alive

and free

like the sun on your face

soft

and slow

but coming from a place

that burns

like my heart for you

in this

moment

I Remember

i remember

your breath

when you came

there was no mistaking

exactly what it was for you

your clothes were still on

but the heat

beneath my fingers

told tales of the explosion

that was about

to occur

and then the moment

the last breath you drew —

your voice

a gasp of disbelief and awe

before your body

began to show us

exactly what it was born

to do

and you came under my

fingertips

but that tiny location

was just a place

on your body

a gateway to the stars

you shuddered

and called out

i swear it was the voice

of god

and you came

again

Pilgrim's Hymn

the pilgrim seeks

only the sacredest of mysteries

as he winds slowly

his way

by trace of tongue

and nose and

lips

from the distant pivot of your ankle

upwards

to the softly-singing valley

that parts its milky shores

inviting his love

like drowning lungs

invite the air

his eyes rarely stray

from yours

his goal is far from riches

there is no thought of fame or

possession

but, this moment,

it is clear

that there is something

that he pursues

there is breath

uttered voice without words

and nervousness –

all that you imagined you'd hear

the moment the door closed

behind him

but these are all things

you'll recall sometime later

in quiet moments

remembering what it was like to be loved

this way:

not for him

or even for you

but as the vessel

of a pilgrim

whose journey found its end

some holy few inches

above your knees

Schoolhouse

i will be the student

and you the teacher

in the little red schoolhouse

of our touching-skin

this ocean world

floats adrift in its own sea of darkness

and the moments are few indeed

when we sit on its shores to ponder

the pointlessness and profundity

of a kiss

so don't be late for class, dear one

the bell is ringing

and in my heart

i only know

how much we have left

to learn

Love From a Barstool

i love you in a way

that confounds what i have come to know

as love

boundaryless

from a place where even time –

the adopted enemy of lovers –

seems disinterested

in seducing my concern

most of us see our love

like a lost and wounded dog

we scoop him up and place him

safe in our care

in a cage

and this is why

we fall victim to

all of those traps

that later make us suspicious

of loving

i love you in a way

that defies that little box

i love you because

i can watch you loving him

the one you've always said you chose

notice as your eyes flick towards yet another

fickleness and fire

and revel in your indomitable wildness

with a smile from my barstool

on all those nights

you barely looked my way

i love you for

the way you won't even kiss me

at first

even though our bodies are well

into the act of loving

because a kiss is the golden wheat-flower

and you wait in patient vigilance

tilling other soils

until it is ready

to be sheared

i know i love you

because my mind —

without once consulting

my will

or my reason —

decided long ago that the truest perfection

in this world

is your breasts

the way your nipples plead

like two impatient children

in the candystore

of my mouth

i didn't choose to make

this discernment

instead

i am its captive

i love you for the way

you get drunk on whiskey

and i get stoned

on your long and longing whiskey-stares

i love you because you barely exist

and then you do again

on my pillows

in the springtime

i know i love you

by the way your fingers cling to me

in the morning

before you've yet recalled

who we are

or the love that you whispered

before sunrise

i don't even know if you remember it all

but it doesn't matter

i used to long for love

but now i just want another cigarette

and another morning

on my back porch

hungover,

tender and alive,

while you sleep soundly

upstairs

in my bed

What Bedsheets Know

there was a time

when i didn't even know

if i would ever again see

your face

but then the universe

in its wisdom and care

showed us that all things happen

just when they should

when we are most ready

to receive

so receive me tonight, beloved

just let me make love to you

just let me make you come

over and over again

once for every lost day that i spent

remembering what it was like

to kiss

your lips

even the poets cannot tell us

exactly what it is like

in those immeasurably-precious moments

when we exist together

not naked on a bed

but alive and pulsing with

the cosmos

so give yourself to me

and i will make you

like a streaming star

across the dark canvas of this night

and my bedsheets

will be the only ones who truly know

what it is like

to be born

as

One

Final Prophecy

Final Prophecy

And now, here at the end, there remains a final prophecy that I might lay at your feet. This journey began with a Personal Prophecy that I called "Dark Heart." I'll never forget where I was when I called upon those words. My mind, in its arrogance, felt untouchable. I thought I had it all figured out. I thought I was safe, a king in his high and guarded tower. I felt like I'd seen enough light that I could dwell in it directly, with no danger of shadow rearing its head again. I was a fool, and this has been my most recent, and perhaps my greatest, teacher.

And so, one day, I called upon the darkness. It was a brash challenge, the folly of a misguided heart, an invocation born of ignorance. In the way a child might chide his playing companions, I cried "olly olly oxen-free!" into the darkness, never realizing that it was listening; not even wholly believing it was there at all. And just as I had requested, the darkness came for me. It was about time that it did.

These past many years of writing have been influenced heavily by this path. Darkness has peppered the landscape of my life, and I have suffered, known confusion, caused chaos, and experienced loss. It's been one hell of a journey. But it was time for me, as it will one day be for all of us, to look at my dark heart in its eyes. It was time to face it down on the battlefield. I do not make the mistake that this path has ended, but I *do* know now what it takes to rise. And here, in this final offering, I share with you what I've learned.

The children's phrase "olly olly oxen-free" has a curious derivation. It comes from the German "alle alle auch sind frei," which literally means "all, all are also free." A more casual translation might read: "All of us are now free." Perhaps it is fitting to end with a final prophecy, one that tells the story of a voyage through terrible darkness. You may encounter it as a personal tale, but the truth is, at the end of our journeys through trial and suffering, we can all bathe in the light of freedom.

Letter to an Old Friend

dear friend:

i've waited long enough

to write this letter to you

just like i requested

my own darkness found me

it didn't take much

just a brash invitation

in a poem that i wrote

thinking i had it all

figured out

on that day, i invoked

the darkness

and it was about time

that i did

once you were a babe in my chest

that i mistook

for a wise old man

there was so much then

that i didn't see

but i understand it all now

i'd spent so many years

climbing that mountain

the journey was perilous and i

had worked so hard

to get there

my legs ached and

my stomach howled

and when at last i reached the gate

it sneered and opened wide

i thought i had reached the end

the stone keep at the summit

had hallways lined with gold

and an empty

jeweled throne

that knew all the right songs to sing

so seduced was i

that i chose to stay

and reign

with no intention of leaving

it is strange to me how foothills

can appear to us

like the tallest mountains

in the range

i suspect that this is how

all the good men

fall

what i should have done

was fill my pockets –

just enough to buy a meal

and fresh soles for my

worn-out boots –

and then set out again

for that peak was just the first

and each night

from my windowsill

i saw the dancing candle-flames

on higher mountain tops:

these were the greater kingdoms

that i chose to ignore

as i went back to the dwindling fireplace

that i tried to call

an inferno

this went on for years

and the people in that tiny kingdom

who once licked sugar from my fingertips

began to grow pale

and malnourished in my shadow

it wasn't long before the pitchfork revolt

and the fires of their torches

illuminated the places

i'd been trying to keep hidden

all along

i ask you, friend,

if you care for me at all

please trust in how much i've seen

and feel my heartbreak

for all the pain that i caused

while sitting atop that false throne

and getting fat

on the bounty of ignorance

i'm leaving now

i'm on my way

i've exchanged my crown for

this peddler's sack

and a beaten pair of sandals

so many would argue that it took too long

but i finally learned that

there is no such thing

as kings

there are only we fools

who mistake a night's respite

for paradise

heart of light

come back to me now

let it be so that i have earned

your faith

you're my oldest friend

and i've taken you for granted

may this letter be a new

prophecy

may new fires be kindled

by our reunion:

the fires of truth

and the cessation of all

my unclear

seeking

in the end

i want you to know that

i've always been wrong about

the long road home –

i guess it never leads us

where we first suppose –

for on the horizon are misty peaks

whose moonlit castles

are calling for us

and the road feels like home

beneath my feet

Acknowledgements

This book was written for you, and I simply cannot tell you how grateful I am that you hold it in your hands today. There are a small number of individuals, though, for whom I have a special kind of gratitude.

Thank you, dear Joseph, my witness and friend, my brother in the Ecstatic Vision. Your wisdom comes like winks that show me what my heart already knows, a loving elbow to the ribs of my Spirit. Your reminder to "never forget the common man's tongue" came just as my words were getting too fancy.

I find myself especially grateful to contemporary scholars such as Coleman Barks and Michael Green. Without their love for and commitment to ecstatic poetry, this book would likely have never been written…and I would still be searching for my Way.

To the community of Berea, Kentucky, I give my deepest thanks. It seems I had to leave home to discover where my home truly was. Berea fashions itself a place where "Art's Alive," and I'm just happy to be living here, for now, learning what it's like to be an artist.

For the past many years, I have been beyond-blessed to have been able to walk the path of the teacher. Lately, though, I've begun to learn the depths of what it *really* means to be a teacher. And on this journey, I have learned that no one is a better teacher than a student. To all of my students, I bow my lowest bow. You are the ones who have worked upon my heart. Thank you for continually showing me my own biases, my blind spots, my hang-ups and preconceptions, and for teaching me how to sharpen my craft.

From the Author

Ecstatic poetry is not new to the world. It existed long before Rumi and Hafez wrote their songs to the Beloved. But recently, change is in the air. Something is happening with ecstatic poetry, as a small part of a larger Whole, at this present time in history. Our scholars are writing new translations, our poets are opening their hearts to their own sense of God and Spirit. We are beginning to respond to the ache, to listen to the cry for peace. We're hearing truth in ancient practices and are reenvisioning them, crafting a fresh sense of awakening for the New World. This is a slow process, and may not bear its fruit until well after my lifetime. But I can feel it happening, even now, and I suspect that you can, too.

My hope is that this work, what I have to offer, will grow to join the multitudes of voices, the congregation of hearts – poets, artists, musicians, storytellers, and so many more – the keepers of peace in these times of warring hearts, warring nations, warring Selves.

I would happily welcome you on the journey of ecstatic poetry, as it continues to take shape as a reinvigorated form of art and spiritual practice in the world today. If you feel inclined, you can follow my future offerings on my website:

www.brandonthompsonauthor.com

and on Facebook:

www.facebook.com/brandonthompsonpoetry

To borrow from Carl Sagan one last time: I'm in love, and I want to tell the world. Come, lovers. Let's tell the world together.

Notes

Notes

Notes

Made in the USA
Charleston, SC
24 February 2016